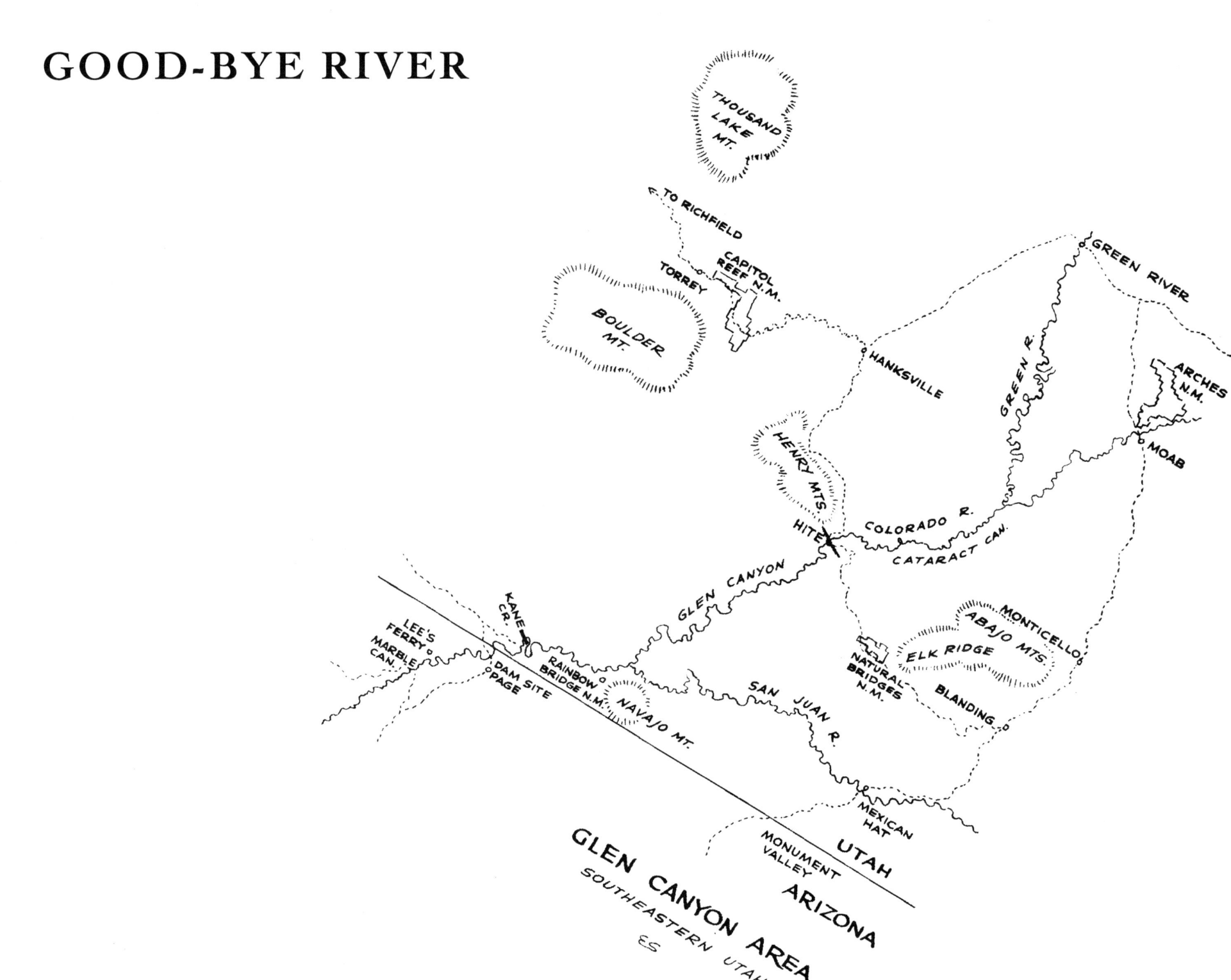

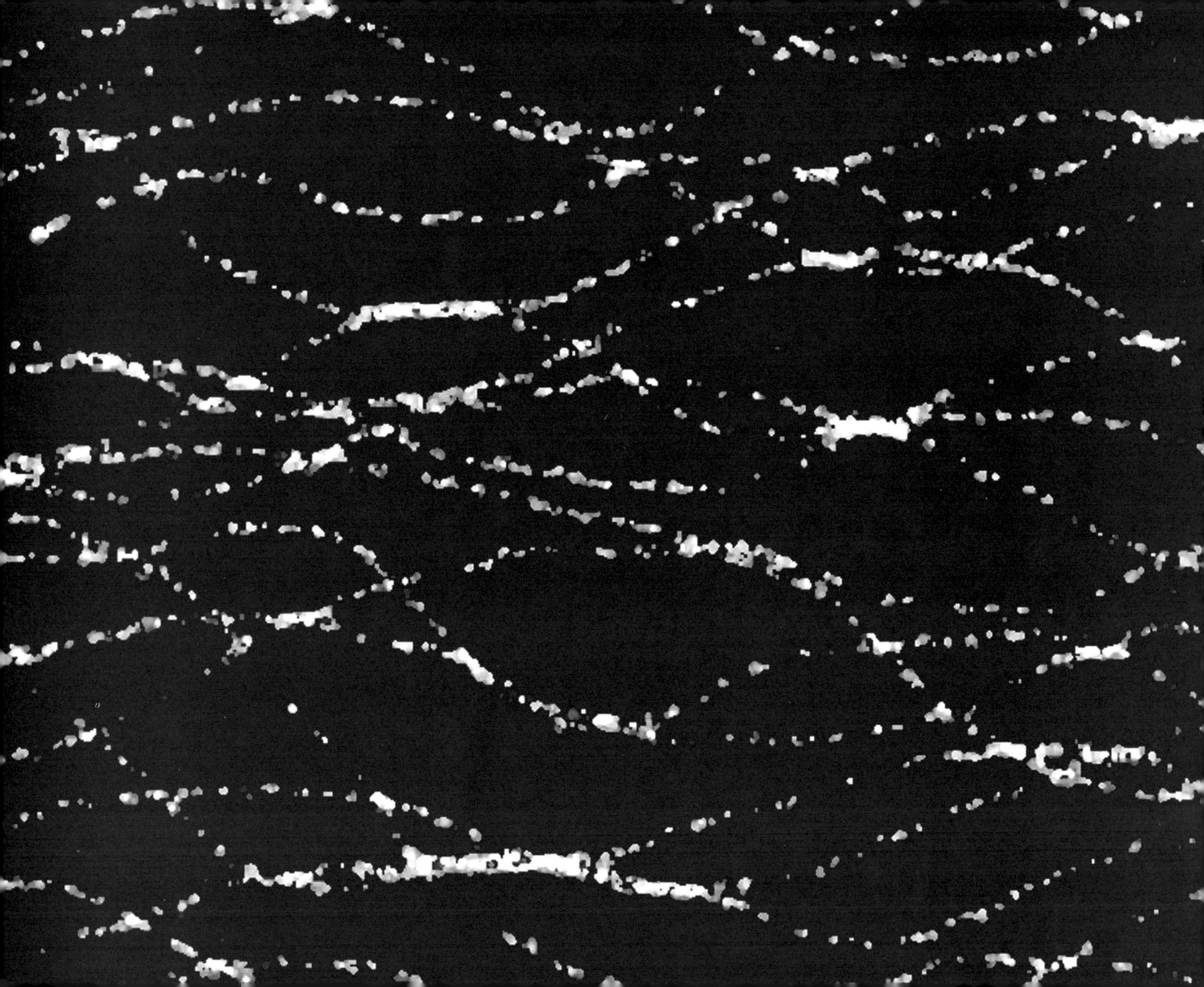

GOOD-BYE RIVER

By Elizabeth Sprang

KIVA PRESS

Las Cruces, New Mexico

Copyright © 1992 by Elizabeth Sprang

All rights reserved. No part of this book may be reproduced or transmitted in any form or by any means, electronic or mechanical, including photocopying, recording, or by any information storage and retrieval system, without permission in writing from the publisher.

Published in the United States by Kiva Press, a division of Shay International, Inc., Las Cruces, New Mexico.

Library of Congress Catalog Card number 92-075575

ISBN 0-9635226-0-4 pt.

Book design and prepress film by
John Cole, Cerrillos, New Mexico.

Printed in the U.S.A.
Printed on acid free paper.

All illustrations are by Elizabeth Sprang except cartoons on pages vi, 17, and 46 are by Dick Sprang.

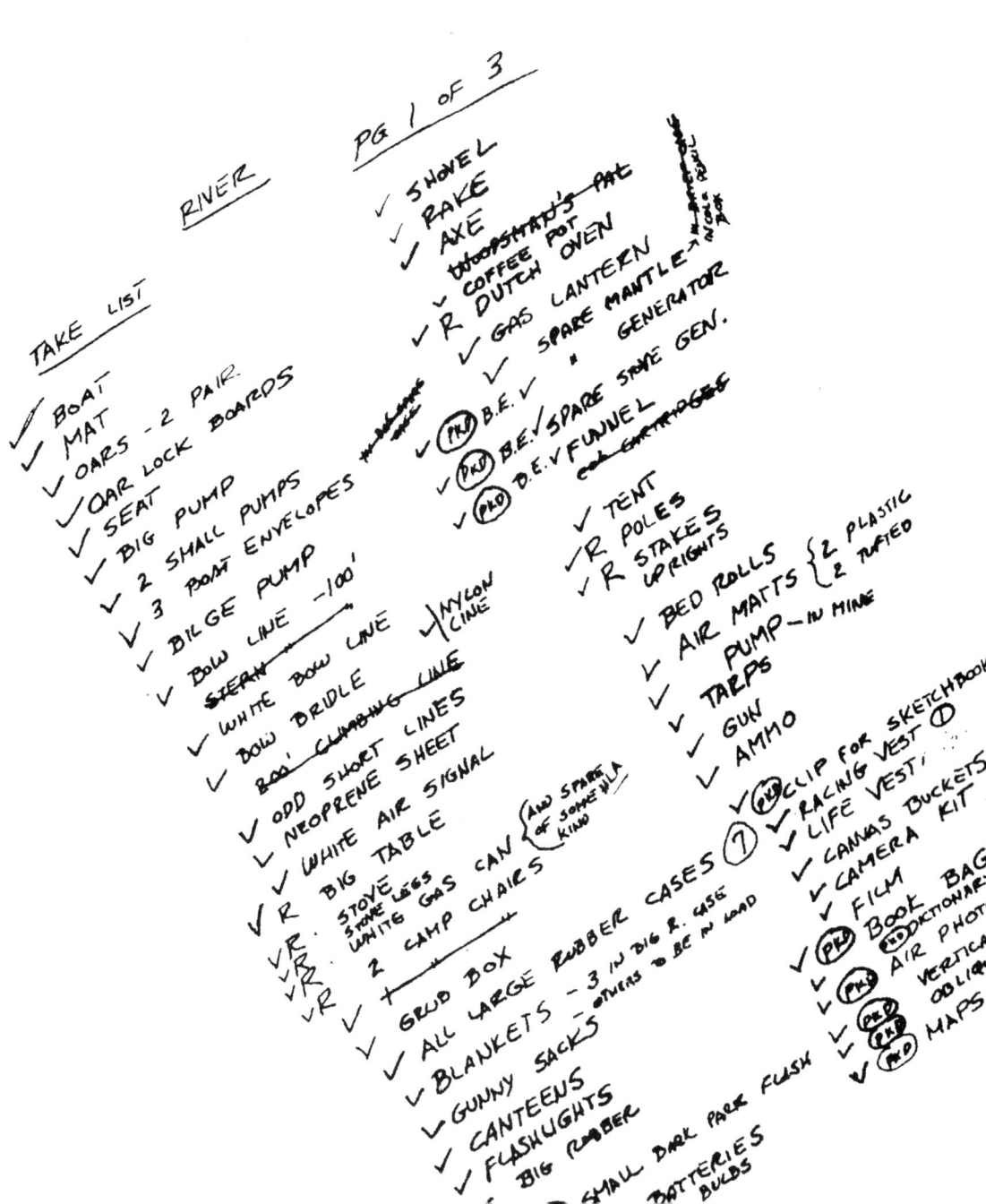

Contents

Foreword vii

Preface ix

Chapter 1 1

Chapter 2 9

Chapter 3 19

Chapter 4 37

Chapter 5 51

Overview 61

Foreword

On the river, the boat stands still. The canyon walls move.
—Elizabeth Sprang, *Good-Bye River*

In *Good-Bye River*, Elizabeth Sprang states without reservation that "Among all the annals of man's stupid mistakes on this continent, surely an outstanding entry will be the destruction of Glen Canyon." This book gives us every reason to agree with that statement.

During the fall of 1959, Sprang rafted the Glen Canyon section of the Colorado River. Not long after that trip, construction of the Glen Canyon Dam began on the Utah/Arizona border. The dam in turn formed Lake Powell, which soon inundated the canyon and, in the process, drowned an unknown number of sandbars and beaches, unexplored side canyons, and Indian petroglyph sites. Large-scale, motorized tourism also was brought to the area for the first time. Since then, Glen Canyon has seen its remaining beaches fouled with trash and human waste, many of its outstanding geological features ruined by overuse and vandalism, and its water employed as a landfill for refuse tossed from houseboats, campgrounds, and marinas.

Thanks to Sprang, we do have some record of what Glen Canyon once was. *Good-Bye River* tells us of the grandeur of the place, of landmarks like Tapestry Wall, a "vertical face, a solid sandstone block a thousand feet high and over a mile long, striped softly with an up-and-down pattern of handsome water stains." With an artist's eye for nuance, Sprang is able also to recall the smaller treasures that existed there:

"This landscape is beautiful
  not only in large design
but in its tiniest details. The
  pebbles, lichen
patterns on the rocks, the ferns
  in the glens, the
driftwood shapes on the shore.

The clean, pure,
unlittered sand is embroidered
  everywhere with
evidence of tiny life: lizards,
  mice, centipedes,
insects, birds."

Though Glen Canyon has been altered significantly since Sprang's last journey there, at least one thing has stayed constant—that being the Colorado River remaining in place while its surroundings are ever-changing. On the river, the boat stands still. The canyon walls move.

America's few remaining wild rivers, especially those in the desert West, are challenged by the human-caused changes and events that continually flow past them. The Virgin River, which winds through the arid lands of Utah, Arizona, and Nevada, is one example of a river that is particularly threatened by the exploding populations and increasing demands of St. George, Utah, and by Las Vegas, Nevada. Already weakened by the impacts of irrigated agriculture and the over-allocation of its waters, the Virgin struggles to provide habitat for a stunning variety of unique fishes, birds, and plants. In fact, some 80% of the wildlife in the Virgin River basin depend directly on the river's riparian zones, although these wet lands account for less than 5% of the basin's total land area. The Virgin also flows through Zion National Park, as well as through several designated wilderness and wilderness study areas, and thus contributes to the region's important recreation economy.

Local water agencies in both Nevada and Utah, however, are developing ambitious plans to appropriate even more water from the Virgin. Unfortunately, water-saving technologies, revised construction and landscaping standards, and other conservation measures receive little attention as plans are formulated. With optimistic growth estimates firmly in hand, these now-booming communities are pursuing increased supplies from a river that barely survives as it is.

Change does not happen to rivers as much as change happens around them. On the Virgin—and on too many other rivers in the world—events are rushing by at enormous speed. Environmental-interest organizations, including the Southern Utah Wilderness Alliance, are working to end the runaway destruction of our waterways. This book is an excellent step toward urging us back to our rightful place—toward returning to a river where one can sit in a small boat, doze in the sunshine, and watch the canyon walls drift slowly and silently past.

Mark MacAllister
Southern Utah Wilderness Alliance/Virgin River Research Project
November 1992

Echando a perder se aprende

"One learns by spoiling things"

—

Old Spanish dicho

Preface

May I add a tiny portion to Colorado River history? Here is my story of a float trip down part of the river before the disastrous Glen Canyon Dam was built.

Yes, Glen Canyon really was like that in those days! I kept a journal. Read it and weep, you who came on the scene too late ever to do the same thing.

Read it and take notice, everyone. Inform yourselves, be aware—lest similar things keep right on happening. "We learn by our mistakes"... unless we decide to ignore them.

—E. S.

Santa Fe, New Mexico
November, 1992

Page 2 of 6
FOOD LIST — (cont'd)

- ✓ 12 Jones Jiffy Meals (gerry) @ 1.25
- ✓ 7 dehydrated meat bars
- ✓ 1 CVC " vegetable stew
- ✓ Egg powder for 32 eggs (1 Tbsp pwd + 2 tsp water = 1 egg)
- ✓ 10 dy heat eggs Soup Base
- ✓ Jiri Tosty Instant Soup
- ✓ 2 Knorr's Egg Drop Soup "
- 16 Wyler's Ham & Lima
- ✓ 2 pkg cabbage flakes
- ✓ 1 ƒL Bean Teaspoon onions
- ✓ 2# mixed k dried fruit
- ✓ 1 qt pure Maple Syrup
- ✓ ft Mormon honey (condensed honey) — need
- ✓ 2# Aunt J. pancake flour
- (Albers buckwheat) "
- ✓ 2# Postum
- ✓ 1 lge MH coffee & 1 small for lunch kit
- ✓ 5 lge ZOOM (6 breakfasts)
- ✓ 1 bx BC Hi Pro cereal
- ✓ 12 bx Sanka
- ✓ 2 # Carnation Inst. nonfat milk crystals (each = 14 qts)
- ✓ 4 lge TANG pwd & 1 sm
- ✓ 6 Rath's LP sausages (have 4)
- ✓ 6 canned fried sausages 1 lge, 3 sm (in refrig)
- ✓ 6 canned hams
- ✓ 4 whole canned chicken (chicken + gt)
- ✓ 2 chicken gravy
- ✓ 2 beef gravy
- ✓ 2# Red Dog flour (El Molino)
- ✓ 3 # whole wheat flour
- ✓ 5

Chapter I

"I ain't afraid of the river, and I hope you ain't, but man, I respect it! You gotta respect it or the goddamn son of a bitch will GET YA!"

—Art Greene

HITE, UTAH, October 4

It is 1959. Evening is falling as we sit on an ancient spring-busted davenport in front of a tent-house among the willows by the Colorado River. I can hear the bells of two black goats that are wandering nonchalantly around on the face of the cliff on the other side and the sounds of a bunch of cows being driven from the area with shouted abuse. Otherwise, the place has been silent all day except for the crashes, bonks, clanks, and grinding roars incidental to the operation of the nearby ferry.

The two of us are waiting to begin a long-planned boat journey down the little-known Glen Canyon section of the Colorado. "Let's go live in Glen Canyon awhile," my husband had said. He is an expert boatman who has been down the river, on oars alone, five times before.

After a month's preparing, we are now ready to put in the river with our neoprene boat and supplies for more than six weeks. Ours is a stout "ten-man" craft bought in 1949 for forty-five dollars at Army Surplus. Originally designed for assault landing on the coast of Japan, it came equipped with a survival kit, which included fishhooks and neat wooden plugs for any bullet holes incurred.

The Colorado is supposed to be one of the world's most dangerous rivers. The part we have chosen to float is regarded as fairly easy and safe. Yet it is isolated, and once in the current, there is no turning back, and no place to get help or supplies.

The one-ton truck that brought us here has gone back to Fruita, 96 miles away, with Malan and Linda Jackson. They will meet us November 15 when we come off the river at Kane Creek, 120 miles downstream, 400 miles away by road. The Jacksons swore we would never be able to get our mountain of food and equipment into the boat! Dick has been working at it most of the day, after the deflated boat was rolled down to the bar, pumped up, and dragged into the water. Tomorrow will bring the test, when the last things are put in.

"This may be the shortest river trip on record!—As soon as the boat was loaded, it sank!"

"But you said it displaces two tons!"

"It's a matter of bulk, too! We might have to camp in one spot and eat and eat till we've reduced the load to a size we can get in the boat!"

Only four people live at Hite now, the Neilsens and, in a trailer-house, a young couple who manage the ferry. The whole place has a certain run-down charm, a deserted end-of-the-world air, as it waits to be inundated by the water behind Glen Canyon Dam, which is now being built. The land and the farms have been sold to the government. The Bureau of Reclamation may soon come in, remove all buildings and steel scrap, and level everything off. Two hundred feet of water will cover the place.

The weather has been perfect today. Seventy-two degrees, windless, balmy. Pomegranates, grapes and jujubes ripening in the Neilsens' garden. Red cliffs all around. The river sliding majestically by, looking

Neilsens' place at Hite, 1959

Chapter 1

very enticing. A drifting boat would progress at a gentle walking pace.

The water is muddy from rains and has a flood smell. This morning about five A. M. I went outdoors. The morning star was brilliant in the east; a bird flew into the willow thicket and lit on a limb close above me. I turned my flashlight on him. An owl! He stared at me and I stared back, until he flew off.

The night was utterly still except for an occasional splashing boom — a peculiar sound caused by a section of bank caving into the river. I also heard a loud coarse cry that must have been made by a water bird: "AAWAAERKKK!" There are blue herons, hoptoads, porcupines, foxes, bobcats, mice, beavers, all sorts of creatures living along the river margins. Ducks and catfish in the river. Most of the birds seem unafraid of humans.

I spent a couple of hours today sketching a marvelously dilapidated lavender-and-green jeep in the Neilsens' yard. Flowerpots, shoes, car parts, and various other impedimenta were piled over it and in it. Reuben and Beth Neilsen appear to be good examples of non-status-seekers. They have lived here for years in a tent-house, farming, developing an orchard, accumulating a fabulous collection of junk, silvery driftwood, timbers fished from the river, broken-down cars, boilers, tools, machinery, engine parts, rocks, petrified wood, purple desert glass, and scores of unidentifiable objects moldering and rusting in heaps among the weeds everywhere. Reuben is foreman at a mine some distance across the river. Disliking city life, he and Beth had meant to live at Hite all their lives. The government will pay the expenses of moving the Neilsens, but they don't know where they'll go when the water comes up over their land.

TICABOO, October 7

Yesterday we got up before dawn, loaded the last things into the boat, and pushed off.

The moment came at 10:30. After snapping a couple of pictures for posterity, we put on life jackets and I crawled into my place in the boat, a hollowed-out nest surrounded by duffel, camera case, tripod, ponchos, backpacks, Coleman lantern box, lunch bag, coffee kit, stove case, etcetera. There was indeed not room for one more item of any size. Dick then untied the mooring lines, coiled the fat bowline neatly in the bow and, as the boat began to drift, leaped in, scrambled to his seat in the cockpit, unshipped the big oars, and maneuvered the boat into the current.

Right away I saw what he meant by telling me, "On the river, the boat stands still. The canyon walls move."

I also noted that an oarsman who knows what he's doing looks relaxed,

Camp at Ticaboo

alert, like he's enjoying himself. Not exerting much strength, he just dips an oar now and then, using the power of the river to keep his boat in position.

An inexperienced boatman, who doesn't keep watch and doesn't know just how to handle his oars or how to estimate the power of the current, may be seen continually struggling —"Always in the wrong place on the river"—rowing for dear life to keep from grounding in the shallows, bumping into the shore, getting hung up on a rock or caught in an eddy.

Unreeling past the boat at two or three miles per hour, as on a conveyor belt, were the colorful cliffs and headlands below Hite. I had hardly time to get used to this effect when we hit the first rapid. Trachyte Number One. It was gentle, the boat just bobbled through, and I found I wasn't scared.

"That's all there is to that."

Soon came Trachyte Number Two and, during the day, a few more easy ones, ending with a fairly bouncy one at Ticaboo. It was fun. The river is about three feet above normal for this time of year, which makes for faster and easier boating.

Even with an upriver wind and a lunch stop, we sped along so fast we made Ticaboo Bar by four o'clock. I don't seem to be very good with the oars, but I am learning how to help with landings. As the boat is skillfully nosed ashore, my job is to grab the mooring rope, hold it coiled just right, and leap onto the bank —whether mud, caving dirt, rocks or whatever—without falling on my face, hang onto the rope, perhaps with a quick turn around any handy object, and hold the boat until Dick can scramble over the load to the bow, jump ashore, and moor the boat properly. Walking around on the boat, by the way, is something one has to get used to; it's like making one's way about on a big squishy, lurching air pillow.

We had plenty of time to set up a good camp in a lovely spot under the willows. Again, the wind died at evening and it was warm as toast. After dinner we sat around the campfire on the beach, glad of the comfortable "officer chairs" that had been so hard to get into the boat at the end. For us, no six weeks of sitting on rocks or cold ground without a backrest!

Getting meals is a breeze, for I have a gasoline stove, work table, eating table, and food cabinet. Before leaving home I organized the first week's dinners in heavy nail sacks, labeled in order, and stowed them in the big neoprene-impregnated waterproof containers. Now all I have to do is get out the sack, open the cans, and heat up and serve the contents with appropriate trimmings. What a wonderful vacation from having to think.

We slept in the open without a tent. Early in the morning I peeked out of my sleeping bag and saw the sky was cloudy, the river a queer milky copper color. A Great Blue Heron flew in, landed on the shore, eyed us, waded on up the shallows looking for breakfast. Later I saw his tracks were seven-and-a-half-inches long.

We slept late and ate a leisurely morning meal. We decided it would be wise to put up the tent, as the wind was rising. The sun came out warm and fine, but not for long. As soon as the tent was up and a fly contrived from a big tarp to keep the wind out of my "kitchen," the wind reversed direction and started howling from upriver. This was supposed to be most unusual.

"We're pitched backwards."

"Well, maybe it'll die down."

After lunch, we walked up Ticaboo Canyon for water and lugged back eight gallons (64 pounds). Up the canyon I took a bath in some natural sandstone tanks hollowed out of the rock by the stream. Saw some fine petroglyphs on a big rock, which will be covered by the waters behind the dam, as will the side-by-side graves of Cass Hite and his partner Delynn, who once had a little home at Ticaboo. (The National Park Service later anchored a buoy over Cass Hite's grave and named the site.) The chimney of their house still stands, and the remains of a vineyard and garden.

There's no way into Ticaboo (Indian word for "friendly") except by horseback or boat. The scenery is like that of Capitol Reef National Monument—red Wingate sandstone cliffs, gray-green and purple Chinle formation below that, with Navajo domes rising far in the distance. Big green cottonwoods and willows. Indian artifacts scattered around.

By the time we got back to camp with the water, the wind was much worse, sending seething sheets of sand off the beach into our camp. Thank goodness the tent was up. We retreated inside to wait it out. It's now seven o'clock. I'm writing this by the light of the Coleman lantern. I'm wondering about dinner. Which method will get less sand into the food: bringing stove and food bags into the tent, or dashing outside to cook and handing the plates in through the tent-flap?

October 9

We ended up eating a huddled-up one-dish meal of canned ham and limas while the wind whistled outside. Then we threw our dirty dishes out the tent-flap to be coped with the next morning, when it would be time to shake the sand out of everything, and zipped up the tent door. Good-night to the world.

"Now you're initiated into the Order of River Rats. That was a regular Glen Canyon blow."

By next evening, the weather cleared up. We celebrated with an elaborate dinner consisting of six hot dishes: corn bread, baked ham, apricot cobbler (made in my first try at Dutch oven cookery), plus cooked fresh cabbage, baked potatoes, and hot coffee.

The next night I daringly tried a loaf of bread, baked in a loaf pan, seriatim with two other dishes. It turned out to look normal and taste delicious.

Yesterday we rowed across the river for exploratory hikes, taking a lunch. Beautiful Chinle formations, weird crusty hills of deep maroon and pale sea-green. Pure white sand beaches, orange and chartreuse tamarisk bushes. Indian arrowhead chippings.

The river has dropped three feet since we camped at Ticaboo. What if we wake up some morning to find the boat high and dry?

Famous last words: "I won't need to wear my life jacket just to cross the river, will I?"

"YES, YOU WILL! That's just the way something could happen! When you're on the river, never make a move without thinking first. When something does happen, it can happen in a split second." The lecture ended with the quotation from Art Greene, a famous old river rat.

Usually the greatest hazards on such a trip are not falling in the river but letting part of a cliff fall on top of you or getting burned handling gas appliances or campfire. You're a long way from anywhere.

Chapter 2

Deep hidden in a land of stone,
Agate, fossil, clay and bone,
  Green brush, green trees,
  A gush of green breeze,
And river's rushing roar forever
Answer the red cliffs' never never never.

Unheeded other worlds, forgot the wise,
Girt by bright fluted walls of paradise,
  Vast and inseparable the days.
  Time goes its ways
Changing minutely things unseen
Till one day all will be as it had never been.

TICABOO, October 10

This landscape is beautiful not only in large design but in its tiniest details. The pebbles, the lichen patterns on the rocks, the ferns in the glens, the driftwood shapes on the shore. It's a delight to be surrounded by such beauty. There are tons of silvery driftwood here, plenty for fires, benches, planks, and decorative arrangements around camp. As for the river-worn cobbles and pebbles, I've gone wild over them, as perhaps only an artist could.

Nearby are big deposits of gravel and cobblestones in a tremendous variety of color, form, and texture. Rocks from Colorado, Utah, and Wyoming, worn smooth through the ages, seem to exude the romance of far places. To handle them gives me a feeling of joy. Some are glossy, plain, perfect; others have amazing designs. There are uncounted tons of them—grindstones, eggs, beans, clubs, manos, cobbles, balls, buttons, hearts, feet, abstract sculptures of all sizes and shapes from pea-size up to a foot long. They are all satisfying to look at, handle, or carry in the hand. To me they are

"..................... dumb
As old medallions to the thumb;
Silent...................... "

yet they speak.

The clean, pure, unlittered sand is embroidered everywhere with evidence of tiny life: lizards, mice, centipedes, insects, birds. There must be lots of beavers, for I see their traces on all the willow banks, where they have dragged willow cuttings down into the water to eat, brought up gobs of ish from the silt to make mudpies, or cut down large trees. I've seen them swimming and heard them diving with a crash. How I wish I could see one close up, but they keep out of sight.

Shapes of stones

SMITH FORK BAR, October 12

Tracks in the sand

*T*houghts. Some people see gold in it, or uranium, or cattle, or tourist profits, but to me, the real lure of this Glen Canyon country is the untouched peace of its yet-untracked plateaus and unspoiled canyons.

This may not last long. Every now and then (and I'm told this was not true in the first days Dick explored the river) comes a reminder of humanity. Big river parties in recent years have set fire to the trees on some of the bars, or put a match to great piles of driftwood, turning the lush greenery at the foot of the cliffs to a charred gray mess. This was done to get color pictures of the flames.

In a few spots, campers have left empty cans, Kleenex, long-lasting Kodachrome foil, toilet paper wads, and other momentos.

Chapter 2

Today we saw a great panel of petroglyphs that had been vandalized. For the purpose of taking impressions, blue latex paint had been sloshed and dribbled down over the figures, permanently spoiling their looks. Earlier comers had crisscrossed scratch marks, carved initials, and chipped off sections to take home.

New roads are constantly being cut by mining or cattle interests. Cow tracks and cowflops are all over.

Even so, we are very far from our usual world. If we lost our boat, it would still be a two or three days' hike out to any place where there are people.

Twice powerboats have gone by, churning up the river—speed! speed!—a painful racket reverberating from the cliffs, shattering a tranquil day where the only sound had been an occasional gurgle of the river, splash of a beaver, or cry of a heron. River rats who depend on oars alone regard powerboaters with the same superior disdain skiers reserve for tobogganers.

Even the sky has been invaded. Evidently this whole great uninhabited plateau is in constant use for military aerial maneuvers and training. Night after night, the darkness suddenly begins to vibrate with the heavy growl of bombers practicing refueling overhead. We stare up at them passing slowly over in pairs like brilliantly lit dragonflies mating.

Will there be any place left?

October 14

We left Ticaboo at noon and made a long haul, aided by some pulling on the oars, to camp before dark on a sandstone ledge just under Tapestry Wall, at Warm Springs Canyon.

In the early afternoon hours it had been blistering hot on the water, probably over 100 degrees. The river was a great glaring mirror reflecting heat. In my thick kapok Mae West I nearly cooked. Finally I got permission to remove it except when landing, casting off, or passing through rapids.

About 3:30, Tapestry Wall hove in view and came silently nearer. Very impressive—one of the landmarks of the river. A vertical face, a solid sandstone block a thousand feet high and over a mile long, striped softly with an up-and-down pattern of handsome water stains.

One overnight camp was spread out on red-bluff rocks on a high ledge above the river. I thought it charming. There was a perfect flat rock

Drifting

table at just the right height. We dined as on a penthouse terrace, then leaned back in our chairs, facing the dark water, to watch moonlight replace the fading daylight, and the moon's path began to twinkle on the river.

We could lie in our sleeping bags in the morning and watch the first sunlight hit the top edge of the Wall and creep down until it hit camp. After that there was no shade; but, before it got unbearably hot, we had loaded up and were floating on down the river.

Now we entered the most typical part of Glen Canyon, full of the glens from which it got its name. The cliffs were beautifully rounded, shaped, and decorated walls of Navajo sandstone, sometimes with Carmel capping. In Zion and Capitol Reef, the Navajo is creamy white and weathers differently. Here it is a wonderfully light rosy-tan shade I've not seen elsewhere.

This day I really began to feel myself to be under the spell of river travel. One of the great joys of river travel, I find, is gazing straight up, up, up at the tall cliffs as they slide calmly by in total stillness. Nothing else is like it.

It's fun to peek up the mysterious crooked side canyons as they pass and wonder what's up in there. Nobody knows; no one person has explored them all.

We didn't row this day, just drifted. At times the silence was absolute. The river didn't make one sound; air and water were still. Then Dick might quietly dip an oar to change direction. The river smelled fresh.

The glens we passed were often sheltered by great blind arches or rock 500 feet high. Inside were air arrangements of greenery fed by dripping springs. Some were like great florists' windows, filled with maidenhair fern, mosses, and flowers. The bars were lush with willows, oaks, and a few cottonwoods. Most of the latter are in side canyons.

These glens and hanging gardens are often under overhangs where rain never comes. Moisture seeps down through the sandstone from above until it hits an impervious layer, then travels to the outside where it drips and dribbles down the wall. Soil forms, seeds find a foothold, plants and flowers appear.

Once we saw a bunch of good-looking mule deer skipping along a talus slope, looking back at us. Once we saw a lone horse posing on the skyline, like something out of a legend. At Olympic Bar we landed to lunch and inspect the structure that had once supported an enormous old waterwheel, built for gold mining, later taken out by flood.

Many are the stories and legends connected with the Colorado, and those admitted to the inner coterie of river people have evidently heard them all. Many are the men who have come here in search of gold, and many have made their mark — an abandoned shack or dugout, a chimney standing stark, a heap of rusted machinery, perhaps a grave. The elite band of river rats who are truly serious about their love of the river are capable of carrying on an endless argument as to whether the cable at the old gold dredge is five-eighths- or one-half-inch thick, or as to what year someone did such and such. Hours are spent discussing history, poring over photos of cliffs that can't be identified, comparing maps, reading each other's river journals, and writing letters to one another about technical points.

I observe also that a terrific professional jealousy exists. Once you've been on the river and enjoyed it, you identify yourself with it some way. It seems like something that's yours alone. You don't want to hear about anyone else's having been to the place you thought you discovered, or having hiked farther up a canyon than you did, or having seen something you didn't see. I notice none of the men can refrain from making remarks about the way others handle their boats.

My own general possessive attitude takes the form of resentment of any man-made intrusion, any desecration, any change in the natural state of things. Also, I hate to see the passing moment pass; I must try to capture it, cling to it, draw or photograph or write, or carry home loot like a magpie to remember it by.

While we were exploring the old waterwheel support timbers at Olympia, we heard a light plane S-ing the river to the north. It was friend Colonel Joe Moser looking for us, as arranged beforehand, to check on our well-being. We gave the "All's well" signal. He dropped a message saying "Have fun" and that his partner would check on us Friday.

We got to Smith Bar later than planned and found the campsite Dick remembered from previous trips to be "gone with the river." Thus we had to camp 100 yards from the boat and carry the stuff a long way, to a spot under a willow tree by the beach, similar to our camp at Ticaboo. As at Ticaboo, it didn't last.

First there was a short reprieve; it was nice next morning. I happily carried all our dirty wash to Smith Fork stream nearby, got it clean, washed my hair and took a bath, scaring all the little fishes into a panic. There were deer tracks all over; the deer probably watched me too.

"Why bother to put up a tent? The weather's perfect."

"Remember, it was just like this before it began to blow at Ticaboo? I'm going to put the tent up."

At noon, the wind began to rise until our beach camp became uninhabitable. Sand came flying down the bar like snow in a Dakota blizzard. Against all rules, it blew again from the north and continued all next day, howling and shrieking its way downriver. We hurriedly moved our table and kitchen to the top of the sand bank, in a hollow among the willows, which helped somewhat. Sand is in everything by now, anyhow. You get used to it! You get in the habit of clapping the lid on all containers the instant anything is taken out.

We had the tent to retreat to, where we sat cross-legged on a sleeping bag eating sardines and a chocolate pudding out of a Mason bottle.

By now we are making great progress toward that real river rat look, authentically beat-up, stained, and ragged. On river trips, the taking of a bath becomes such a momentous event that I see that people always note it in their journals! Some dispense with baths altogether. Every piece of clothing that can give way, wear out, fail,

Colorado River Adventurer as imagined by the public

Colorado River Adventurer as encountered on the river

or disintegrate does so with great rapidity. Hair hangs in strings; beards grow untamed. When civilization is reached, people sort of peer at one, in a way which is rather ego-satisfying.

Yesterday the wind was still blowing. We hiked up Smith Fork, a long and very beautiful side canyon, as far as we could get by lunchtime. The backlighted cottonwoods made startling clashes of green against glowing apricot walls. The light seemed to bounce and reverberate from one side to the other. In places we walked as though suspended in orange luminosity. There were glens, glyphs, Moqui walls and a granary, a mano, an arrowhead, a metate.

Wednesday the wind quit. Now we can live in comfort anyhow—we have a windproof camp in a "hole" chopped out of thick willow growth.

It's been getting colder and colder of nights. Twice it was at 38 degrees by the camp thermometer when I struggled out of my bag in the morning and hastily yanked on clothes over my pajamas so not to lose that precious layer of warm air! By about ten o'clock it warms up, and I change to

Chapter 2

lighter things. By noon it's around 70 or 80 degrees, which means in this thin air that in direct sun it's really boiling hot. When the sun goes down, the temperature instantly drops. We build a fire and/or put on more wraps. All this seems to involve an unconscionable amount of time spent putting clothes on and taking them off.

Harry Aleson, a well-known riverman, is said to have licked this problem by dressing over his pajamas when he first got up, then by removing layer by layer as the day warmed up, until he was prancing around the bar in polka-dot pajamas, sun helmet, beard, and camera. Later he would add on.

We have a modish split-level camp here, which complicates life. Cold air is supposed to sink, isn't it? Well, it doesn't here. On the beach below us tonight it was a balmy 65 degrees, while behind up on the bar in our camp kitchen it was 45 degrees. By noon we're sizzling hot, surrounded by buzzing flies as we eat lunch. By dinner we're shivering, dressed in five layers, while I keep gloves on to cook!

We've developed real river appetites by now. Whenever a recipe says "Serves four to five," I know it will be enough for two. I don't think we've lost any weight. Friday night we had another Dutch oven jamboree, plus (courtesy of Oak Creek Flying Service, i.e., friends Joe Moser and Ray Steele) fresh T-bone steaks, ice cream, beer, and a bottle of Jim Beam for Dick. It wa very exciting when the plane zoomed in on schedule. Dick had staked out a white sheet for "All's well" and flashed the plane two heliograph signals.

Joe is commander of an air rescue squadron, and Dick and Ray are fliers. The men seem to get a big kick out of doing everything according to the book. Should things turn serious, they are prepared. Had we given the prearranged signal, "HAVE LOST BOAT, CANNOT PROCEED," or "NEED MEDICAL HELP, MATTER OF LIFE OR DEATH," a helicopter or motorboat would have appeared within hours.

Chapter 3

Long ago I loved to stroll among the hills
  and canyons,
And take my pleasure roaming the wilderness...
Wandering to and fro amidst the hills and mounds.
Everywhere around us are dwellings of ancient men.
Here are the vestiges of their walls and hearthstones,
There the smoke of their fires has blackened the roof
  of a cave.
There one has patiently chipped a design on the
  smooth rock,
Yonder chipped arrow points, or ground-out corn.
I stop and ask a potsherd gatherer:
"These men—what has become of them?"
The potsherd gatherer turns to me and says:
"Once they were dead, that was the end of them."
In the same world, men now lead different lives,
Some in government, some in the marketplace.
Indeed I know these are no empty words:
The life of a man is like a shadow-play
Which must in the end return to nothingness.

—with apologies to T'ao Ch'ien

October 19

I'll never forget these radiant October days in the Canyonlands. Already a week has gone by at Smith Fork. One feels one could stay here forever.

Nights we sit by the fire on the riverbank to watch the moon rise over the ink-black silhouette of the rims of Forgotten and Bobtail Canyons. A wide trail shining like molten lead is reflected on the broken water. The sound of the rapids is always audible here, clear back to the cliff where the glyphs are, behind the bar.

Days we explore the bars, benches, and canyons. Sometimes I sketch. At night the moon is so bright I could sketch by its light, and once I got up in the middle of the night to do it. The rapidly changing shadows on the infinitely subtle modulations of the sandstone nearly drive me crazy. We did take photographs, and I made rubbings and drawings of particularly nice petroglyphs nearby.

Looking across the river from Smith Fork Bar

Evenings we sometimes climb up the talus behind the camp to watch the sunset view downriver. In the mirror glass-like water are reflected faraway cliffs, and beyond them, distant blue peaks of the Waterpocket Fold—far, far away—so far, so tiny, so perfectly drawn that, like a cloudcastle on a summer's day, they seem to hold all the magic of that unattainable land of dreams where everything is peace and perfection.

This whole trip continually brings home to me the truth of some sayings of Dean Brimhall, a retired psychology professor I used to hike with in Fruita.

"This is one of the highest forms of reality."

"You can't understand this country until you get it into your muscles."

"Experiments with dogs have proven that if they have one place to stand where they are safe from conflict, they can better withstand neurosis-producing stress. It's the same with humans. Some people take refuge in music, or religion, or stamp collecting. With me, the place to stand is nature."

Twice we took lunches along and spent the day on the far side of the river. We equipped as for a safari,

Moonlight on the Colorado

Turner's name misspelled on handmade concrete headstone

with a heavy-caliber gun at Dick's hip in case we met a wild bull. One had actually charged a man on horseback near here and put him off his horse.

Forgotten Canyon was a disappointment because the pottery shards and chippings that used to litter the ground when Dick and his party first investigated the prehistoric ruins years ago were all gone. Mass river parties had picked up and pocketed every one. The ruins had been dug and left a mess by University of Utah archeologists. The oak groves on the bar had been burned.

Bobtail Canyon, next door, was an experience to remember. Its entrance was a place of such entrancing beauty, I have no way to evoke it with the worn words of our language. A grand old cottonwood tree, rugged and muscular, arched backward out of a dune, like a guardian spirit at the entrance. A silent river of apricot sand of the most delicate shadings flowed out between towering walls. The cliffs zoomed straight up, each patterned differently: one in vertical stripings, one in rich Oriental tapestry, another in sculptured bas-relief featuring soaring sea gulls' wings. A place of unmarred magic, totally pure, where one could dream of staying forever enveloped in pink silence.

Monday we walked in the footsteps of the Moqui. We climbed up over the Navajo domes and California Bar acoss the river to foray into another kind of world. It was a relief to get up high after being down in the slot so long. As we climbed, we found ourselves using old footholds chiseled in the rock centuries ago. They go clear to the top. When spring floods made the lower route through mud and brush impassable, the "old people" evidently used this high route around into Forgotten Canyon. There seems to be no difference in the culture between the two sides of the river, so they must have had a ford just above here.

The highest point we reached gave a wide view of the river. Apparently the old people liked to enjoy the scenery as they worked, for there was a "spalling anvil" where the old Moquis sat and whammed out chunks of arrowhead material by pounding them on a big boulder. The marks on the rock were still there, and chips and flakes still lay on the ground.

Everywhere were remains of ancient terraces where the river had been cutting milleniums ago. Some of the gravels from those days have lain stranded on the sandstone in the sun, rain, and wind until they are scorched dark by desert varnish, polished almost like glass. Arranged in little gardens, set with pristine perfection like showcases bedded in red sand, or scattered artistically on smooth rock, with here and there a tiny cactus, Indian chippings, or sandstone marbles mixed in, these pebble gardens fascinated me so I could hardly be dragged away.

These gravels also contain veins of flour gold. Away down California Bar we saw the workings of an abandoned gold mine. A fellow by the name of Turner lived there for many years, worked the mine, built himself a cobblestone house, and when he died, was buried there (by request) in a lonely grave. Arthur Chaffin fashioned a headstone from cement.

The setting is stupendous. Despite the summer heat, Turner must have loved the place. His little house is in ruins now. Iron objects stand about rusting. Gold-washing machinery, a winch loader, an old trunk, a washtub, purple glass. Above, the great arched cliff. A canyon entrance with cottonwoods and a clear stream. The great river flowing past below. The whole scene could be painted in just three colors: burnt sienna, black, and white.

Turner cabin ruins, California Bar

October 20

*T*oday we hiked upriver on Sundog Bar, climbed the cliffs, and roamed around on the slickrock for hours. We finally reached a point 720 feet above the river, according to the topo map, where the whole country opened to view. The huge landmarks of Navajo Mountain, the Henry Mountains, and the Kaiparowitz Plateau rose blue on the horizon.

This whole magnificent Utah country does force one to keep in mind the inconceivable immensity of time and space, the cycle of geologic forces, the measureless sweep of existence, compared to one person's life span. In the city one is so well surrounded by the works of man, one falls into the habit of assuming they are all-important. One is enclosed by other people, a sort of mutual entente is formed wherein it is assumed that man's importance and ability to comprehend are unlimited. Not here.

Consciousness of the unknown, of the country as an "X" factor outside human control, is noticeable in the conversation of the natives. "The country" is something that must be considered in all calculations.

Here one also realizes something else, a thing often forgotten amid the conveniences of civilized life: how we are basically dependent on the sun! After shivering around in the predawn hours a few times, waiting for the appearance of that warm, sovereign, blessed giver of all life, one understands why the "primitives" worshipped the Sun.

On this kind of trip one realizes, too, why this sort of interim is good for the "civilized" soul. One is forced to think, not of silly abstractions such as filling out forms on paper or adding up columns of figures, but of concrete matters such as simple survival! Survival this minute, too — not some later minute or some hypothetical minute. No problems exist that can't be coped with immediately; no anxieties that can't be worked out in action. One is forced to live in the here and now, out of doors in the open air, physically active all day, as human beings were probably intended to live when they first came off the drawing board.

This thought came to me today while edging around a tricky slanted rock shelf high above the river. Of course, I realize what we're actually doing on this trip is having the best from both worlds: eating our cake and having it too—getting an atavistic joy from sitting around the campfire, then using a Coleman lantern to light the way to bed.

Up there on top of the slickrock plateau, we found no intrusion of humanity whatever. Here at last was the true, pure primeval world.

A vast humming silence hangs over it.

I felt half afraid, half enraptured as I moved across it. The slickrock is marvelously solid and satisfying, a joy to walk on. Of course some of its slopes are impossible; on some, one's feet can barely stick. But in places one can march for miles insect-like over the vast convolutions of bare rock, staring around at the strange scene. Here and there are gathered in hollows, little colonies of balls, like marbles, from pinhead size on up.

They come from concretions, embedded in the sandstone, which gradually weather out through the years and roll down until they catch somewhere.

One also sees weird remnants of formations that stick up or lie around like prehistoric monsters, dragons, or lizards. Horrible outsized twisting potholes disappearing into the depths now and then scare you from going near, for fear you might slip. What a fate that would be!

One thinks, "Nothing could live here! We have penetrated beyond the pale!" Then suddenly appears a miniature world of green hidden in a depression that holds run-off water through the year, cottonwoods, and a pond. We came to such a pool, concealed in acres of bare rock, just when I was beginning to wonder how much longer we could go without water. The canteen was getting very low. We were dehydrating by the minute. But I wasn't sure I wanted to drink from a stagnant-looking pool inhabited by a crowd of green trilobite-shaped amphibious creatures about an inch-and-a-half long! On the shore at the edge of the pool, some of these peculiarly repulsive armored tanks were constantly fighting viciously, rolling over and over, waving their many legs and whip-like whiskers.

Dick poohpoohed my attitude, saying, "If it wasn't good water, they wouldn't be living in it." He lay down on his stomach to drink, then brought me a cupful. I had to admit it tasted heavenly.

But how did the living creatures get there? And how does the water in these pools on the slickrock stay fresh and ice cold, as it does, all through the hottest summers?

The immensity, the coloration of the slickrock country, the experience of walking over it, seemed to have no relation whatever to our usual world. Just pink-tan sandstone rolling to the horizon in folds, domes, chasms, ridges, canyons, subtle modeling, and contours of exquisite gradation. While through it all, under the saturated-blue sky, at the bottom of the slot the river has carved, the great calm opaque greenish-brown Colorado flows.

Back at Smith Bar that night, having negotiated the descent from the top of the cliffs, I thought how lucky the "old people" were to have lived their

Hunch-backed flute player petroglyphs

Bird petroglyph

Chapter 3

lives in such an environment. It reminds me of the famous Navajo prayer:

In beauty may I walk,
  All day long may I walk,
  Through the returning seasons
    may I walk....
  With beauty may I walk.
  With beauty before me may
    I walk,
  With beauty behind me may
    I walk,
  With beauty above me may I
    walk,
  With beauty all around me, may
    I walk.

The momentos these ancient people left behind them are—unlike ours—all beautiful things to see. They were always embellished with a true artist's touch, a bit of decoration unnecessary from the standpoint of function.

One can't help but feel they appreciated the harmony of the whole when one sees at the bottom of the great cliff wall back of camp, pecked in the dark varnish of the ages, man's

Chapter 3 29

Copying a design from a rock at Ticaboo

30 **GOOD-BYE RIVER**

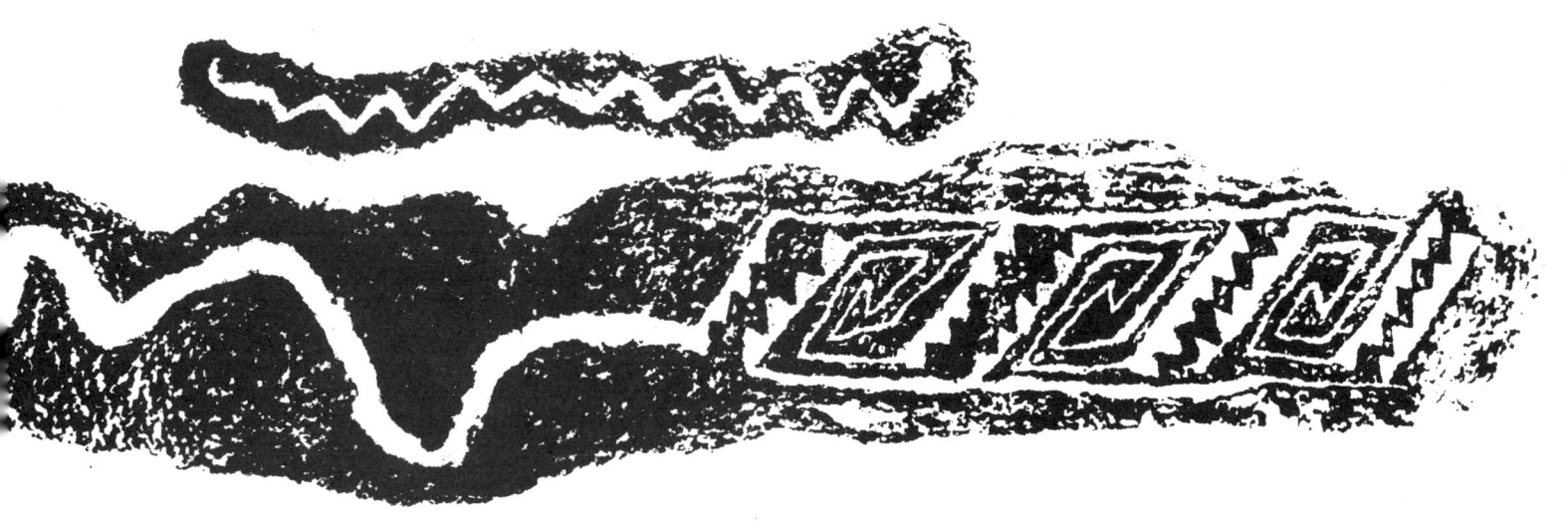

GOOD-BYE RIVER 31

Petroglyphs, Smith Fork

creative statement—a neat abstract design six or eight inches high and ten feet long. (Years later I learned, on the authority of Jose Arguelles, that this "fringe motif" is a universal symbol of creation found throughout Central and North America.)

There is also a little-known picture of the famous humpbacked flute-player incised in another spot on the same dark red wall. (The flute-player, like all symbols, is a double or triple entendre. According to Arguelles, one of the presently understood meanings is that he is the culture-bearer who brings people out of their caves.) And there is a depiction of a man drawing a bead on a mountain sheep with his bow and arrow while a friend impatiently dances up and down nearby.

These were discovered by Dick, in addition to the big main panel of petroglyphs that everyone who stops at Smith Bar walks back to see. Knowing it would not be long before they were inundated, I made rubbings, sketches, and photographs of everything there was time for. Our week at Smith Fork is drawing to a close. It will soon be time to take to the river again.

HANSEN CREEK BAR,
October 22

Before leaving Smith Fork Bar, we spent one whole day in camp organizing gear, washing clothes, taking baths, and cooking up Dutch oven breadstuffs for the journey.

This camp was hard to leave. When I woke Dick by stirring around in the chill of dawn on the day of departure, he protested sleepily, "Why do we have to leave? It's all right here."

We'd stayed so long and our stuff had gotten so thoroughly scattered, it took till noon to get packed. When we got going, we drifted for 45 minutes through the calm, perfect afternoon, landing here on a rock ledge above the river—a cozy, convenient camp. Back of us is a fallen-down dugout fireplace and a rusted boiler lying on its side with a pack-rat nest in it and bobcat tracks over the top.

This is said to be the remains of a camp where some Japanese once worked the bar for gold. On the cliff behind are incised the first good white man's glyphs I've seen on the trip. They are dated 1898.

BULLFROG BAR, October 24

*W*e are here instead of at Moki Canyon, where we had planned to be. We wanted to camp several days there and explore old living sites, but when we tried to land, we ran into problems. Instead of the beach that had been there before, there was deep, gooey mud, and a high bank tightly interlaced with willows. We did manage to get the boat tied up to a root and fight our way by inches up the slippery bank on our hands and knees, only to find the old campsite ruined. Again, someone had set fire to the trees. The whole grove was charred black, the ground covered with ashes.

   We lunched, filled our canteens, and left to look for a camp farther downriver. On a sandstone ledge about a mile beyond, we made a "throw-down" camp without water or wood.

Since it was still warm and lovely next morning, we got inspired to reorganize the whole boatload. At this point it was apparent I'd brought far too much food, and Dick suggested we cache some of it, plus some of our loot, at Hall's Creek, where we can later retrieve it by jeep overland.

After sorting the containers spread out on the rock and after repacking, we drifted about 40 minutes more down to Stanton Canyon, opposite the mouth of which is an old gold dredge wrecked in the river. After investigating and rejecting the possibilities of a camp there, we drifted on in the evening shadows and finally pulled in at the one spot (we later discovered) on Bullfrog Bar where landing could be made. A fine spot, with a bronze sheerwall rising right behind us, lots of driftwood, and water only 15 minutes away in Bullfrog Canyon. The temperature stayed at 60 way after sundown. Only drawback: no shade. But we were on our way before the sun got high.

Chapter 4

Stone within stone, and man, where was he?
Air within air, and man, where was he?
Time within time, and man, where was he?

—Pablo Neruda

HALL'S CROSSING, October 25

This is a really stylish camp—looks just like an ad for Abercrombie and Fitch (except for the characters inhabiting it!) Surrounded by big old willow trees leaning at picturesque angles and dripping feathery curtains of greenery, we can look northwest through orange tamarisk plumes toward the Waterpocket Fold. Southward we look across the river and up, up, up at a stunning 500-foot sheerwall of dark red rock, which keeps the camp in shade all day. Between the camp and the cliff lies the river, gliding in such total silence I forget it's there. Everything is still with a stillness that doesn't hum as it does in the heights above.

Ranged in a handy ring around the fire are tent, kitchen, wash table, clothesline, and easy chairs. Near the center is the dining

Luxury camp near Hall's Crossing

table, covered by a snazzy red plaid cloth. A Coleman lantern is set in the middle. Dick is studying maps there and checking Gus Scott's and Harry Aleson's river journals.

For this model camp we have even cut dandy steps down to the boat landing, laid willow cuttings in the sand for a rug around work areas, and hung a decorative string of flags that came tied to Moser's airdrop. It's 60 degrees tonight at nine o'clock; we can sit out here instead of crawling into the tent to keep warm, tent warmth being provided only by excess heat thrown off by the Coleman lantern. It's very cozy inside as long as it's above freezing outside.

This fancy "home away from home" was achieved by a rugged process of selection. We first drifted down from Bullfrog, landed, and scouted twice to inspect possible sites. We hiked across acres of slimy boulders and sand, fought our way through thick tamarisk forests, and slogged over sand dunes to get across the mouth of Hall's Creek to the entrance of Lost Eden Canyon and beyond. No soap.

The only item of interest we found was an old Mormon inscription incised on a sandstone slope: "R. Blackburn, Dry Fork, Uintah Co., Utah, Oct. 14, 1905." Mr. Blackburn must have been pretty homesick, and he must have had a lot of time on his hands. He had painstakingly carved a house with chimney, windows, steps and door, put a frame around his name, and added a nosegay of flowers. On a nearly ledge, Dick found a chisel made from the tang of a broken file which fitted the grooves of the inscription perfectly.

Rock inscription, Hall's Creek

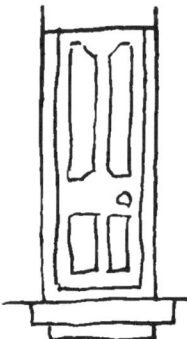

A little higher upriver is a well-known place on a vertical wall chiseled with many historic names, including Howland's. I later made rubbings of these.

This camp has only one drawback: there's nothing to drink except muddy river water. Most river rats drink it without hesitation. One of them, Dock Marston, ended up submitting to an operation to remove the silt from his insides.

There's good water in Hall's Creek, but the carry would be a mile round trip. We do have eight gallons left from Bullfrog, however, and we'll drink that and use river water for washing. It settles out fast. We have a neat row of canvas buckets set out to settle on the bank by the steps.

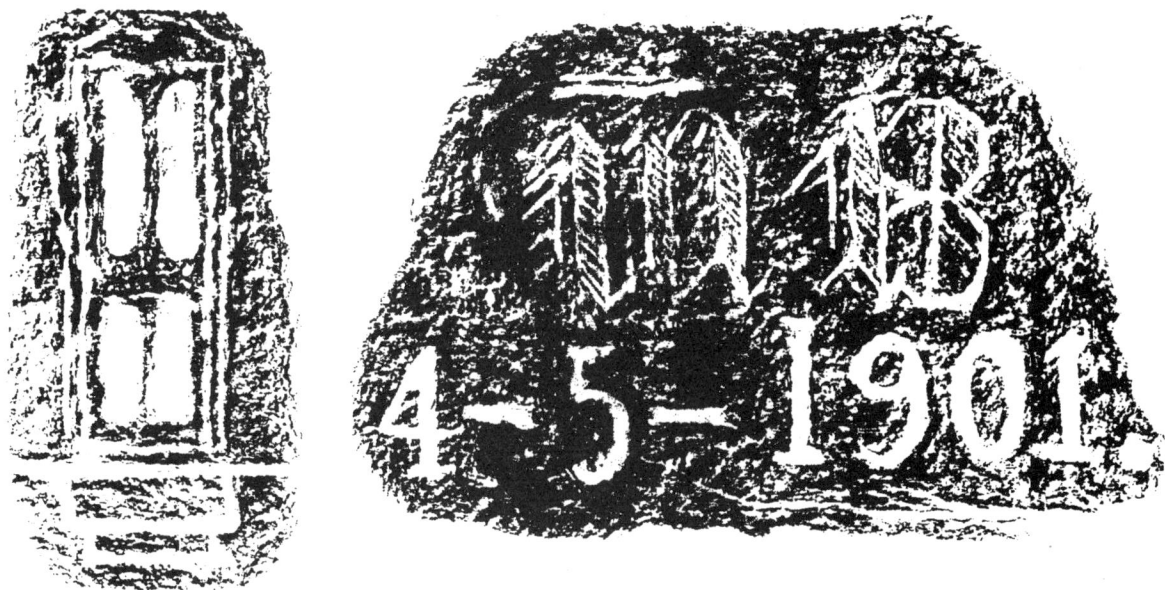

October 26

𝓐 lazy day in camp. Temperature not above 70. Cached our stuff and scouted out a route for the jeep when we come back to get the things. This involved hiking up a steep historic road, once used by wagons coming to Hall's Crossing. One can still see the grooves marring the sandstone where the wheels dragged coming down. Cairn markers have been built on the trackless portions of slickrock, so modern jeeps can find their way. Dick reset many of them. (We did come in by jeep overland in May, 1960, to pick up the stuff we had cached.)

At the top, the view opened out into one of the most vast imaginable. Truly awesome. "Makes Capitol Reef and half the other National Monuments look so sick you wonder why they kept them and let Glen Canyon go to pot!" The lonesome Henrys and Navajo Mountain were on the horizon as always, and westerly we saw the Waterpocket Fold.

Hall's Creek

When we got back to camp about five, it was such a warm idyllic evening we heated up some settled river water on the campfire and took baths. Before dinner, Dick brought out the bottle of Jim Beam, airdropped by his friend, and drank a toast.

Next day we hiked out on top once more. It had started out to be a shadowy gray day, with splatters of rain, but soon clouds broke up and the sun came out. We didn't dare cross Hall's Creek for fear it might flood and maroon us; it was obviously raining somewhere on the watershed, and if the creek rose, we could be stranded on the wrong side for days without food or shelter.

Hall's Creek flows at the bottom of a meandering stone trench so tremendously deep as to make it inaccessible from the rim, all the way from its mouth nearly to Baker's Ranch. At the mouth is a wide expanse of mud and slipperycobbled boulders, at best difficult to negotiate.

In fact, this whole country has Jekyll-and-Hyde aspects. Wallace Stegner called it "a lovely and terrible wilderness." The expanses of Glen Canyon along the river borders do contain warm, intimate scenery where one can feel at home. People have lived here for centuries, and one senses this, as though their spirits still lingered. Glen Canyon, as Stegner said, is "absolutely serene, an interval for pastoral flute." One is happy on the sunny bars, among the willow greenery, the caves and ferny glens with trickling water, protected by the canyon walls.

But the higher one climbs, the more one gets the feeling that nature is inimical. On top one walks in an impersonal wilderness of stone that seems to have no possible relation to human life.

I can't think of any adjectives except over-used ones: unrealizable, fearsome, awe-inspiring, grand. The sweep of geologic time that went into the making of this scenery simply can't be grasped by the human mind in its present stage of development. Even the half-realized intimation of it makes a shadow of chill vertigo slide over the soul.

It is alluring and repulsive. Crawling like an ant among the massive stone furniture of this plateau, one feels that in a twinkling its strange beauty could turn to horror. (Mountains above timberline, though I love them, strike me the same way). A slight change in the weather—a wrong turning—an accident imperiling life—illness, depression, or exhaustion that alters perspective—and suddenly! the bald stone becomes ugly, the steep slopes where no feet can cling menacing and sinister, the great gruesome potholes frightening, the distances wholly impossible of accomplishment. . . Often the wild wind moans and saws and howls; always it is an enemy.

In summer, the heat radiating off the slickrock can kill. Among canyons that look identical, one could easily lose one's way, for mile upon mile there is no water at all, and nothing green, no plants except cactus, grass, and yucca in occasional depressions. When anxiety changes the aspect of everything, one wanders beleaguered in a hostile world.

October 28

𝒜fter a clear morning came an ominous change: a few breathings of breeze that rattled dead willow leaves onto our camp. The wind worked up to gusts and whirls that roared straight down on us from the cliff, ruffled the river, and sent the sand up into tschindis (dust devils). The sky clouded up rapidly and turned blue-black in the northwest. The temperature dropped 10 degrees. After last evening's silent electrical storm, now thunder began muttering and mumbling around, echoing among the cliffs.

Right now (6 P. M.) it's raining. We have battened the hatches with tarps and rocks on everything in camp and crept into the tent, set for a wet and windy night. With all the stuff we've brought in with us, there's hardly room to move. The best idea seemed to be to curl atop sleeping bags and write up our journals.

Today we had visitors, the first humans we've seen in three weeks. Dick talked to them; I was off sketching. Two young fellows from the Fish and Game Commission were making their first trip down the river in a motorboat. They were quite thrilled by it all — but couldn't figure what anybody would be doing on the river for five whole weeks!

They said it was planned to fill Glen Canyon Reservoir (Lake Powell) very slowly. It is not expected to be full until 1971. If there are drought years, it will take longer. The lake will have 1800 miles of shoreline — it will be the third largest reservoir in the world. Hall's Creek will be the second biggest estuary usable for fishing purposes and will be made into the center of a big recreation area. Wahweap-Warm Springs will be of first importance.

The lake is expected to be full only 15 percent of the time. The rest of the time, of course, it will look as any lake does after it's been pulled down a few times: the margins will have a deposit of gunk. With the vast sweep of water and the violent winds that occur here, terrific waves can arise suddenly. Tragedies are bound to occur. A good deal of time will have to be spent rescuing people or fishing them out of the lake.

Taming the mighty Colorado, I guess, is quite a thing. Its average annual flow is 12 million acre-feet.

Silting is one of the worst problems dam-builders face. Past a fixed point at Bright Angel Creek the river moves from one to 27 million tons of sediment every 24 hours. Right now the river is higher than usual for this time of year, running 600 cubic feet per second. During the spring floods it can run 200,000 second-feet; in the past it has run as much as 300,000, way over the top of the streambank willows under which we've been camping.

Its basin drains one-thirteenth of the United States, or 250,000 square miles. The upper basin, above Glen Canyon Damsite, drains 110,000 square miles. From its source to the sea, the river drops 6,000 feet.

While Glen Canyon is regarded as the most scenically beautiful part, Cataract Canyon and Grand Canyon offer the greatest challenge to boatmen. Until 1927, Cataract Canyon claimed the lives of one-third of all those who tried it.

Lost Eden Canyon

The once-unknown section from Green River, Wyoming, to Callville, Utah, was first navigated by John Wesley Powell in 1860. His party made the trip in four rowboats, never knowing what to expect around the next bend.

Rights to the runoff from the river were allocated in 1922, in a compact affecting the upper-basin states of Utah, Wyoming, Colorado, and New Mexico, and lower-basin Arizona, California, and Nevada. The states have been squabbling about it ever since. Had it not been for population increases and ineffective conservation measures, there might have been enough for everyone.

Among all the annals of man's stupid mistakes on this continent, surely an outstanding entry will be the destruction of Glen Canyon. One wonders at the mental processes behind spending millions to drown that priceless canyon to make an ugly fluctuating reservoir and silt depository to prolong the life of Lake Mead to generate more electric power for burgeoning population areas (when we are already moving into the age of atomic power) and to bring upstream diverted water to submarginal farming regions (when farmers in well-developed areas are being paid by the government not to raise crops).

No negative pressure was brought; no voice was raised in protest until it was too late. One reason may have been that Glen Canyon was so little known by the general public that, when the Sierra Club and other conservationist groups fought to preserve Dinosaur National Park, it was agreed to let Glen Canyon go—a political exchange. Nobody pointed out that, of the two, Glen Canyon was far superior.

CHAFFIN BAR, October 29

Summer has fled. We are stormbound in an old miner's cabin on Chaffin Bar, said to be the only habitation with a roof in the entire length of Glen Canyon.

At Hall's this morning we crawled out of the tent to find camp in a soggy condition. The rain and wind had stopped, but because of the shadow of the cliff, the sun never hit camp to dry it out. We had to build a bonfire to dry things and scrape the mud off them before we could break camp. This took until quarter after twelve.

How good it felt to get out of the shadow and drift in the sun once more! But soon a chill breeze rose. High clouds diluted the sun's warmth. Cumulus clouds that had been hanging sullenly on the southwest horizon still hung there, looking sinister. We decided to keep going and look for a good place to camp as soon as possible.

Shallows kept us from landing at Lake Canyon. Farther on, we stopped to inspect and reject a campsite on the opposite side. We finally had to make an 11-mile run, longest so far, before reaching Chaffin Bar.

Although he had never seen it, Dick knew there was an old cabin somewhere on the bar. Arthur Chaffin had offered him the use of it in case of need. At the moment, this offered possibilities of an answer to prayer. We landed on the first possible place on the bar two hours before dark. The cabin was not visible from the river.

Dick scouted and found it almost immediately. A little path had been cut through the willows from the beach to a dilapidated rock hut, roofed partly with tin, partly with boards covered with tarred carpeting, the whole roof weighted down with rocks.

He brought the boat down to be moored in front of the cabin. The beach was so shallow there, he had to wade back and forth in icy water to unload. By now it was beginning to sprinkle.

Interior of Chaffin's cabin at midnight

46 **GOOD-BYE RIVER**

I inspected the cabin. It had one door, a screen door hanging open. Mice and birds had been going in and out freely. Inside was a dirt floor, four rock walls, a fireplace, and four glass windows. Two of the walls were actually the bedrock of the ledge against which the shack was built. For this reason, the floor varied in level two feet from back to front. The only furniture was a plank table, which we promptly put the kitchen cabinet on. We hung a blanket over the door to keep out the wind, and shifted things around so that, for a while, none of the roof-drips landed on the things Dick was bringing in from the boat.

Now, after dinner, all we have to do to retire is fold up our eating table, find a place to stash it, and unroll our sleeping bags on the level spot where the table had been. How lucky we are—this dump seems like heaven tonight, with the wind sighing and the rain rattling on the tin roof!

It seems an interesting bar, and we've decided to stay here a few days, perhaps hike out on top. The bar is two miles long, with beautiful glens and caves in the cliff behind. I found a piece of river-rounded wood on the beach. Mine workings and rusty machinery are all around.

October 30

Come bedtime, it began to rain really hard. As soon as we had our beds laid down in the only possible place in the mousy-smelling dust, the roof-leaks got really started. One began to drip square on Dick's forehead as he lay in bed. He promptly donned his sun helmet.

BAP! . . . BAP! . . . BAP! . . . resounded, echoed by PLOTCH! . . . PLASH! . . . PLOP! all around the room.

"This is the Chinese water cure for sure," were the last words I heard as I pulled my tarp clear over my head

Cliffs behind Chaffin Bar

to keep out the splatter and died to the world. That night I was so tired nothing could have kept me awake.

About 2 A.M. I roused to find Dick still stirring around nervously with a flashlight, chewing nuts and candy, adjusting the tarps as new drips appeared, and worrying about the boat's getting loose from its mooring. He finally got up, dressed, and went out to look at the situation. He ran another line from the boat up to a tie on an old embedded railway iron right in front of the cabin door.

As the night wore on, one could hear above the noise of the rain a tremendous roar upriver, as the whole non-porous landscape began to run. This morning, it's still wet, gray, windy, cold, and disagreeable. This fact can't be evaded: a general storm has moved in from the north.

October 31

*L*ater that day it cleared enough for us to explore behind us on the bar, where there's a fine tall waterfall. The stream runs down to pools close by the cabin, a wonderfully handy place to get washing and drinking water.

Then it began raining again. About three o'clock it cleared long enough for the tent to be pitched on the flat in front of the cabin. Dick also pumped out the boat, which was ankle-deep in rainwater. Nothing was damaged; now is the time when those pesky rubber containers, so aggravating to undo and fasten up again, really pay their way. They can lie and soak in water for weeks, and the contents will emerge dry as a bone!

We haven't stopped thanking our stars we made it here before the storm hit. We continue to enjoy the use of the cabin as a cook-and-dining shack, but we sleep in the clean tent. How wonderful to have our neat little home back again! By this time, we were both more exhausted than we knew. We went to bed at nine o'clock and were still in bed at nine the next morning.

November 1

Still grim, gloomy, and overcast this morning. River still rising; our boat, which had been hard aground, is now afloat. Groups of ducks and flying wedges of big gray and white geese fly past southward, QUANK-ing loudly. The beavers are ker-PLUNK-ing in the water nearby. Fresh deer tracks are everywhere around us.

Yesterday on a stroll down the bar, I found a mano laid in place on its metate, and a couple of pocketfuls of chippings and broken pottery blackened in the campfires of the ancients.

I did a wash, made an ink sketch of the cliffs downriver, and cooked three large meals plus a backpack lunch for tomorrow, when we intend to climb out on top via an old dugway by which a bulldozer was brought in about 1938. Dick worked on his journal, carefully refigured our schedule to Kane Creek in the light of bad weather, reorganized the boatload (a recurring occupation), and made a crazy cartoon of our Dirty Little Hut in the West.

Chapter 5

[The Plateau Province is]... "a great innovation in modern ideas of scenery... the lover of nature, whose perceptions had been trained in the Alps, in Italy, Germany, or New England, in the Appalachians... or Colorado would enter this strange region with a shock, and dwell there for a time with a sense of oppression, perhaps with horror... Great innovations, in art or literature, in science or in nature, seldom take the world by storm. They must be understood before they can be estimated, and must be cultivated before they can be understood."

—Dutton

November 3

We expected the weather to clear next day. A prolonged rainy spell in October in the Canyon Country is unheard of. Not one of Gregory's books, for instance, mentions the possibility of such a storm. But when we woke next morning, there was no sun, it just kept getting darker and darker, and soon after we set out on our hike it began raining again, much to our disgust.

"It NEVER rains like this."

We were wearing waterproof rain-jackets, topees, and carrying light packs. The idea was to trace out the old dugway and get high enough to at least see the Hermit Lake area as well as the familiar landmarks. Because it wasn't raining very hard (yet), we kept going all morning. A mile up the bar, we walked past many caves and boldly striped cliff walls. There were marks of Caterpillar treads and grooves made by its temblebug. They could be traced to the spot where they came off the slickrock onto the bar twenty years ago, in getting into the "goddamnedest place a bulldozer ever got into."

One of the men who worked on that job was later quoted as saying, "It sure was hard work getting the damn thing in there, but I never had so much fun in my whole life!"

Climbing higher and higher, we kept searching out the dugway. It continued to rain gently. We looked for a cave in which to eat lunch. Found a fairly deep one, where we could sit dry inside the drip-line. We ate, looking out through a clump of scrub oaks to a pool. It began to rain harder. We waited a while to see if it would let up.

After about an hour, without the slightest preliminary warning, there was a shattering crash of spume and foam. A full-grown waterfall suddenly leaped out full-bodied above us, landed on the oak thicket, cascaded into the pool, and roared on down over the slickrock.

"How could it start so suddenly?"

"Someplace just got full up and spilled over. It's still raining and still running."

It was, indeed. The fall kept gushing down full force, beating the leaves right off the oak bushes. After watching this and marveling for some time, we decided to go out and look around. We had no desire to get caught out on the bald rock in a genuine cloudburst, but what was happening?

And that was the time we entered the "World of the Waterfall"—an experience rare and unforgettable.

Everything in sight was running—the whole world was running in sheets of water as off a tin roof. It was savage, wild, glorious. Fantastic as a fairy tale or one of Poe's horror stories. (Where did I read of a castle chained to a ringbolt in the rock in the middle of a cascade?)

Under the misty sky, the wet sandstone turned sheeny and pearly-toned. Where it had been hot and dry were rushing lacy-white cascades, foaming streams, churning pools, curving and spouting aqueducts and waterfalls of all sizes thundering into plunge basins until the whole world was one big roar.

A waterfall that always stays in the same place is worth some oohs and aahs, but one that appears dramatically out of nowhere is even more enthralling. When falls appear all over the place, right in the middle of a dry landscape, the effect is really thrilling.

Across the canyon, the great cliff walls were sheer to the talus. Threadlike spouts began to appear at the summit, first gauzy and waving in the wind like the Bridal Veil at Yosemite, then reaching white ropes all the way down. First one or two, then many more. When they hit the talus, they divided and poured in many streamlets down to the river.

The rain kept beating down. As we walked down the expanses of smooth rock, rushing sheets of water spouted up against our legs. By now we were so sopping, we just merrily sloshed along through it all—following the old "cat" route, higher and higher, until, as the afternoon began to darken and the clouds closed in, we realized it was getting to be quite a long way back to camp. And—would we be able to get across the torrents that had sprung up behind us?

It turned out we had no trouble, though it took a long while to get back home. We had to stop often and stare awestruck at the spouts of water booming over cliffs that had been dry that morning. Unbelievable how they roared!

To me, this demonstrated once and for all how all those handsome black and tan vertical stripes got there. The Navajo sandstone in Glen Canyon, unlike that in Zion and Capitol Reef, contains manganese and iron which, in solution, make a stain. I also saw in living technicolor how the plunge basins form. The basin back of Chaffin's cabin was being further rounded out and eroded that day by raging clouds of spray and spume that made an incredible disturbance—and vanished next day, along with all the other waterfalls.

When we got back to the cabin, the wood was wet, so we couldn't have a fire. I had turned into an icicle by now and had a hard time getting warmed up. Is it one of nature's laws that the choicest experiences are reserved for those who can stand discomfort? Why? Because then one appreciates them the most? Wandering that day in the cold and rain on the bald rock had been a dream-like, wondrous thing.

HIDDEN PASSAGE, November 6

Next day, November 3, we thought surely the sun would shine. But no—not for more than two hours. Then came more clouds. More rain. More wind. We tried to get our camp organized to leave the next day if the weather made it at all possible. If we don't keep to our schedule, search parties will be sent out.

November 4 the river had risen a foot and had become very muddy. The weather did not look good, but we packed up and left. The morning sun was soon obscured by clouds. The cold wind grew nastier and nastier until it got really uncomfortable on the river. Howling gusts struck the boat and made it hard to control. To keep the boat from being driven ashore onto the rocks, Dick sometimes had to row until he was gasping. At times the wind would blow the boat back upstream, or crossways of the current. In these river winds, any object left loose will go a-whooping. But this is nothing, Dick says, compared with some of the storms that hit the river. Whirlwinds can take everything in camp and hurl it straight up the cliff! Gusts can blow the boat bumbling against a sheerwall and scare you half to death!

There was a good current, and with Dick rowing nearly all day, we made 16 1/2 miles. Rowing kept him warm, while I stayed cold, bundled up in everything I had plus layers of blankets.

We made a quick throw-down camp on the left side of the river below Rincon at Mile 91.5. A big colorful tamarisk sheltered the tent somewhat from the biting gale. We cooked inside the tent. It froze before dawn; there was ice in the canteens. At intervals all night one could hear wind roaring down the river canyon like a freight train.

During the day, we had met three people coming upriver in a motorboat: Jack Brennan taking two Bureau of Reclamation men to check section corners. They all looked blown to pieces, blue-purple, and half-frozen.

Since there are no more "interesting" camps after we pass Rainbow Bridge and since the weather promises to be nothing but an endurance contest, Dick was inspired to send a message via Jack to Art Greene at Wahweap, asking him to pick us up with an outboard motorboat at Rainbow Bridge camp five days from now. Towed by a motor, we can make it the rest of the way in half a day instead of four days.

November 5 the weather did clear up, but it never did warm up noticeably. Whenever the boat drifted in the shadow of a cliff, we felt the instant chill of winter. We glimpsed Navajo Mountain—and it was white with snow from top to bottom! Boulder Mountain and the Henrys must be covered too. We've been caught by an early cold spell.

Except for historic Hole-in-the-Rock, the section of Glen we passed through next was rather uninteresting. I couldn't help thinking what it must have been like for 80 wagonloads of people to spend the winter on that narrow ledge beside the water. Not far beyond that, we passed the inconspicuous entrance of the San Juan River, one of the most isolated major river junctions in the United States.

As the sun got low and began casting red evening light on the cliff, we drifted round a bend and saw approaching an absolutely spectacular campsite—the most beautiful of the whole trip.

Of course, other people had camped in this setting, but there was no sign of humanity there now. A lovely clean rock shelf to set our tent on, surrounded by big rocks (which always make me feel happy), and a view of towering Navajo formations that outdid everything I'd

Hidden Passage

seen so far in majesty and power. I've tried to sketch them—hopeless. Tried to photograph them, but can't get one-quarter of them into the finder. How can I let this passing moment pass? I would like to keep it forever.

But we could stay only two nights. It's a fine camp from a practical point of view, with pure spring water near, good driftwood for fires, Moqui caves (lately excavated), glens hung with ferns (as well as poison ivy).

Our little lighted tent, shining in the middle of the big black wilderness, looks romantic as all get-out with the moon sinking over Hidden Passage.

Last night was so cold I got chilly in my sleeping bag for the first time on the trip. Tonight Dick wore his down jacket to bed, and I put on two layers of clothes. From now until the end of the trip, I intend to keep my long underwear on at all times. It's the only way! The hardest time comes when one has to crawl out of a toasty sleeping bag to "step out of the tent" at 5 in the frigid morning. The stars are brilliantly polished then.

Today would have been a divine day if that measly earnipping little wintry breeze had ever stopped. We spent some time getting food and stuff organized for the next couple of days, which are to include an overnight backpack trip to Rainbow Bridge.

This isn't a stylish camp; we have left much of our junk in the boat and make do with the basics. I love this place because it's untouched, pristine. When we sat by the campfire at dusk, a fearless mouse darted out of the rocks, ran in and out all around camp leaving a lacelike trail in the sand, scurried over the chairs, looked everything over. He didn't move if you reached toward him. I came within an inch of touching him when he ran over a chair beside me.

There's no sentimental nonsense about "dat ole man river" here. When I was getting out of the boat yesterday with an armload of things, I dropped a jar of maple butter, and the river snatched it in a split second.

Below the mouth of the San Juan, it seems siltier, full of sand-boils, sand waves, and eddies. Not that it ever was a thing to fool with; it just seems less so now. Quite a lot of drift is going by. Judging by deposits high on shore, the spring floods must bring ten to twenty times as much water through, along wih all kinds of debris, including full-grown trees. The current is so fast then that one can get from Hite to Kane Creek in a few days. Dick says that in flood times, the river humps up in the middle like the crown on a highway, and you have to fight to keep the boat from sliding off the hump.

Hidden Passage camp

WAHWEAP, November 12

From Hidden Passage to Forbidding (Aztec) Canyon was an easy eight miles. We arrived by early afternoon, despite the usual nagging upriver wind. We stopped once so I could see Music Temple. Farther on, we found a warm protected spot with a rock fireplace and a wood table, among the tamarisks, and pitched camp leisurely, to get ready for our Rainbow Bridge hike the next day.

Hundreds of people have camped there—it's where everybody stops. For many years Art Greene has run trips upriver from Wahweap to show people Rainbow Bridge. The big share-the-expense river parties always stop there too. Though the Park Service constantly polices it, the canyon is trashed up.

Next morning, as the stories say, we "shouldered our packs and took to the trail." It was so cold, we had to add the extra weight of heavy clothing. Dick's pack must have weighed three times mine, since he insisted on carrying my air mattress and waterproof ground cloth as well as all the dehydrated food, first aid stuff, and incidentals.

I was in pretty good shape by then, but found it a hard hike owing to the irregular going and heavy packs. Many stream crossings; much balancing and climbing over boulders, sand, and slick algae-covered rocks. Much climbing up and then walking down again, all in a deep canyon in the Navajo. Bridge Canyon, the fork in which the Bridge is located, has an amazing slotted entrance. Beyond, the icy-pure stream runs through natural "tanks" or "tubs." Strange symbols and numbers have been painted on the rock by engineers surveying for possible dams and tunnels to be built to protect the Bridge from damage by the lake. (A poor idea, it seems to me, for they would cause more ecological damage than they would prevent.)

At last, around a bend appeared frosty Navajo Mountain. And there was one end of Rainbow Bridge, back-lighted beautifully by the lowering sun. Soon we were in view of the whole thing—a perfectly proportioned arch of rosy-tan stone, soaring up, amazingly large and high. In the same way that Gothic cathedral arches do, it gives a lift to the spirit.

Many, many people had camped right under the Bridge, as was obvious from the debris. We hurried on, to get to our campsite before dark. There was supposed to be a "place in a cave" higher up, where Bill Wilson of the old Rainbow Lodge on Navajo Mountain used to camp all his dudes overnight. At the foot of the Bridge, Theodore Roosevelt's name and many other famous ones are in the register. In the old days, it used to be quite the thing to take a 15-mile horseback trip in to see the Bridge. The Lodge is now burned down. Sightseeing parties now usually approach by water.

We found Echo Camp to be sheltered in a perfectly enormous glen containing a dry waterfall over 100 feet high. We slept almost under the arch of the undercut cliff. It was like being down in the bottom of a cold damp well. A porcupine kept grunting and rooting around in the tin-can pile all night.

Pack rats rattled the dishes we'd left out. It was so wet and cold that I put my bedroll on top of a table. Dick finally got up and built a fire.

The camp did have a lot of conveniences, including a clever stone fireplace, wood ready-cut, plank table and benches, three cots, two big cabinets full of food and dishes, two Coleman lanterns and a Coleman stove—with gas in them!

I can tell you that we were long gone from that camp before the sun hit in the morning!

Back on the river by early afternoon, I rested while Dick reorganized the boatload for an early start the next day. The boat was due to pick us up next morning. We were ready by nine-thirty.

We waited around until eleven before deciding to head downriver under our own power. After about an hour's rowing, we thought we heard the roar of a motorboat coming, but it turned out to be a plane—Ray Steele with a couple of passengers. Our boat was hidden in a bend, so they nearly passed us by. Dick caught them with his signal mirror. Ray turned, zoomed low, dropped something on the bar we were passing, and flew on upriver.

We hastily landed. Dick charged all over the bar before locating the drop. It was T-bone steak again, beer, and a note from Joe and Donna asking whether we were ready by now to "subject ourselves to modern conveniences."

ARE WE READY!

We lunched there on the bar, then continued downriver nine miles from Aztec before meeting Earl Johnson's boat. Jack Ray, assistant to the area supervisor for the Park Service, had come along for the ride. They brought us up to date with gossip and tidings from the outer world, including the news that Art Greene had just gotten married again and was in Phoenix on his honeymoon.

The men hitched the boats together side by side, and we proceeded to chug downriver, getting stuck on a sandbar every now and then. The river was falling fast, and channels were constantly changing—in fact, in places there was no channel.

It was a lovely ride, as that part of the canyon is most handsome, expecially as late shadows fall. We landed at Kane Creek at 4:30 P. M., November 11.

I discovered that, although we had managed to keep track of the calendar, my watch had gained one hour during the month we'd been away from clocks.

Leaving most of our stuff in the boat, to be unloaded the next day, off we went to Wahweap in a four-wheel-drive vehicle. Earl had waited for us. The twenty-mile drive took an hour and a half. The country we went through was out-of-this-world beautiful—first in the pink-and-blue dusk, then in the light of the rising moon. I was happy to be in the back of a truck, with no roof—my favorite place to ride.

Here at Wahweap, I have met Art Greene's family, all old friends of Dick's. We have three whole days to rest up before Malan and Linda are due to come for us with the truck. Never were modern appurtenances so appreciated: we live in a luxurious trailer-house, with bathtub, shower, heaps of hot water (imagine), and enjoy delectable meals cooked by somebody else!

November 13

While here, we've had a chance to inspect Glen Canyon Dam site and the construction town of Page that has sprung up on a desolate plateau across the river. Business is moribund right now, construction on the dam has stopped because of a workers' strike, and Page is nearly deserted. Earl Johnson also took us for a ride past Marble Canyon to Cliff Dwellers on Highway 89, owned by more of the Greene family. They have found, and mounted on the walls, the best collection of arrowheads I've ever seen.

Park Headquarters will be right here at Wahweap, where the Green family has the concession for a lodge, motel, restaurant, and river trips. A few years from now, this spot will be right on the shore of the new lake. It's expected that it will surpass Grand Canyon in number of visitors.

Wahweap is a high, soul-satisfying place to be for anyone who loves tremendous vistas, sweeping lines of plateaus and mesas. One can see 180 degrees of far, far horizon. From the front windows of our trailer-house, we can watch the light change all day on the formations up-country toward Navajo Mountain, sleeping blue on the horizon. From this viewpoint, no one could guess that a great river is hidden down in the bottom of a slot in those mysterious plateaus.

The fabulous buttes and escarpments that look like a dream picture of Zane Grey's ideal West perhaps will look even more fantastic when a blue lake lies at their feet. Changed, unnatural, but still beautiful. When I get furious at man's wrecking nature's beauty, I ought to remember more often that things go always in cycles, that nature renews herself endlessly. "Unto the place from whence the rivers come, thither they return again."

Day after tomorrow, we leave for home.

Good-bye, Glen Canyon, good-bye.

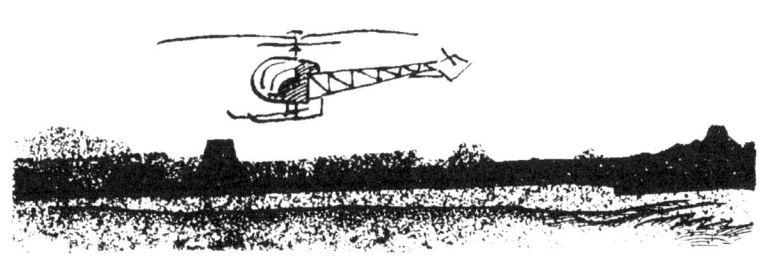

Overview

"Generations have trod, have trod, have trod;
  And all is seared with trade; bleared,
    smeared with toil;
And wears man's smudge and shares man's smell;
  the soil
Is bare now, nor can foot feel, being shod.

And for all this, nature is never spent;
  There lives the dearest freshness deep down
    things. . . ."

—Gerard Manley Hopkins

It is 1978. The dam has been built (no one can quite remember why), and the river no longer runs. A lake more than 180 miles long covers its channel. The Glen Canyon we knew was lovely—but it no longer exists. The two people who shared the adventures in this book have gone their separate ways. The endless flow of change and creation has brought all sorts of unexpected things.

So why look back?

To learn something? To understand the present?—for the past is really part of the present. To marvel at the contrasts, to stand in awe of the possibilities?

Yes, Hite is under water. So are Smith Fork, Hidden Passage, and the Crossing of the Fathers. The cottonwoods are long drowned. Where did all the beavers go? Lake Powell is nearly full, lapping so close to the abutments of Rainbow Bridge that a person can walk to it in five minutes from the landing dock. There are five marinas, the largest one at Wahweap. Huge campgrounds serve thousands of vacationers who rent boats or bring their own to enjoy the lake. Fast highways now crisscross the canyon country, making minutes out of days the old-timers used to trek. Wilderness travel has become a different experience from what it used to be. It is no longer possible in America to be alone in the wilds for long periods. That possibility has been replaced by one of comradeship and interaction with a variety of people met along the trail. One can only pioneer under the sea or in outer space—either of which requires team effort.

Most of the old-time rivermen are gone. Their place has been taken by big commercial outfitters with motorized neoprene rigs, who make a business of taking large parties river-tripping—so many, and with so much publicity, that the National Park Service has for years been forced to ration the number of people going through Grand Canyon, for instance.

Even in 1973, an incredible 14,145 people took trips down the Yampa and the Green. Boating has become so popular that people haul boats clear across the country, from as far away as Florida and Oregon, to play on Lake Powell. Some hardy souls are seeking wild rivers as far away as Mexico, Canada, South

America, Nepal, and India. Some of the adventurous are roaming the far corners of the seas in small boats.

On the limited remaining wild rivers, demand for guided trips is becoming so great that squabbles and lawsuits are inevitably arising between the special-interest groups involved. Suits are being brought in Arizona and California to determine whether commercial operations should continue to be given precedence over amateur river runners in the national parks. (In Grand Canyon National Park, the concessioners are being given 92 percent of the user-days allotted. Of individuals applying for the remaining 8 percent, nine out of 10 must be turned down.) Meanwhile, the Sierra Club is filing suit in behalf of the Grand Canyon, alleging overuse due to "environmentally damaging" contracts between the National Park Service and the concessioners. And the Wilderness Public Rights Fund is filing suit alleging that no commercial operations should be allowed until the demand from individuals is met. Four noncommercial river runners are joining the WPRF in a case now before the Ninth Circuit Court of Appeals alleging, among other things, that the Fifth Amendment is being violated by the government's imposing different regulations on different classes of people (those who can afford a guide and those who can't).

The Colorado Plateau Province is still there, but the crystal purity of the air is gone. This happened faster than anyone imagined. One has only to fly over Utah and Arizona to see, year after year, dirty smog closing in the horizons, filling the depths of Grand Canyon, and obscuring Navajo Mountain.

Pollution billowing from the stacks of plants at Page and Farmington fouls the air over four states. In fact, it is the only man-made thing visible on earth from outer space. Five ever larger synthetic fuel plants are projected for the Four Corners area. Massive strip-mining and transport of coal and uranium is planned, with creation of great new boom towns, threatening destruction of the way of life of the Navajo people. The region has apparently been designated for "national sacrifice."

Why all this—seemingly typical of a world-wide trend?

Gas and oil, food, water, and space are getting short at a time when most national birthrates are not slowing, and all peoples are demanding an equal share in opportunity. But shortsighted political decisions, mismanagement of environmental and human resources, overpopulation, and pollution are not really the most immediate global menace. The crucial fact is that commercial greed and ego-driven power conflicts are now combined with the galloping spread of atomic weaponry.

Neither signs nor prophets are lacking that our particular cycle in world history could come to a very sudden end. At the same time, portents can be seen for another sort of future.

The current moves faster and faster. In just the few years since Glen Canyon was spoiled, man has reached the moon and walked on it. The children of the Atomic Age have entered the Space Age and the Age of Aquarius. Not only has our species split the atom and escaped the boundaries of our planet, but it has also cracked the DNA molecule code and has made other tremendous discoveries, some dealing with the origin of life. Visionaries are talking about space migration, psychokinesis, astral travel, and communication through psychic energy. In a sudden explosion of interest, we are learning more every day about the powers of the human mind and spirit. There is a growing sense of unlimited potentialities.

It is beginning to be realized that inner space is as infinite, multileveled, mysterious, and important as outer space. The old subject-object concept doesn't cover the facts. The universe (including ourselves) is, in this view, not a conglomeration of separate parts, but a series of living, ever-changing, interlocking, self-organized energy systems cycling forever through the process of life-death-rebirth.

These ideas have been around for thousands of years. It's what the mystics have been telling us all the time. Holistic concepts are intrinsic to American Indian, Hindu, Tibetan, Buddhist, and other cultures. But now our physicists are talking in the same framework. This concatenation is new. Perhaps no society ever before had the opportunity to combine spiritual insights with such a great range of scientific and technological knowledge.

Old concepts are being discarded so fast that it seems we may be on the verge of one of the quantum jumps of history. The results could be beyond present imagining.

It's hard to believe a species capable of such achievements as ours could be anywhere but at the beginning of its journey. There may be millions and millions of years ahead of us in which to evolve. As Don Juan said," Our lot is to learn and to be hurled into inconceivable new worlds."

When our present environment gets jammed full of people, there is still the refuge of the boundless inner world. Once a person (by whatever method) gets a vision of the cosmic web of which we are all a part and understands the interdependence of everything, he will live differently ever after. Will enough people reach that level in time?

The trouble is, the knowledge of non-separateness, leading to compassion for others, can't be derived from propaganda, preaching, coercion, or change of political systems. Reading or hearing a million words means nothing as long as the ego is in the way. Transformation must be personally experienced at a profound level.

Only then can we discard the old motivations of greed, egotism, and jealousy. Only then can we figure ways to divide the limited resources of the globe in enlightened fashion.

It can be done. It could happen. It may not happen here, or in time. The denouement of the drama is hidden. It will be the inexorable result of countless actions or non-actions taken by each one of us, all over the world.

If enough selflessness and scientific know-how were to be practiced on a daily level, it would naturally and easily become a priority to avoid damaging each other or our environment.